EUCLID'S HARMONICS

Jonathan Morley

ink
sweat
&tears
PRESS

Published by Ink Sweat & Tears Press
London SW12 8DG
inksweatandtears.co.uk

© Jonathan Morley 2016
Series editors: Kate Birch and Helen Ivory
Designed by Starfish Limited
Typeset in Monotype Baskerville
Printed and bound by Page Bros, Norwich
Cover image derived from John Speed's 1610 map of Coventry
Photo of Holland's memorial plaque courtesy of Jason Scott-Tilley

John Hewitt quotations in 'The Silver Age' and 'Note on The Silver Age',
from 'Art Room in a City School', *The Collected Poems of John Hewitt*, ed. Frank
Ormsby (Blackstaff Press, 1991), reproduced by permission of Blackstaff
Press on behalf of the Estate of John Hewitt.

ISBN 978-0-9927253-2-7

FOR COLIN AND DELIA

Philemon old and poore
Saw Baucis floorish greene with leaves, and Baucis saw likewyse
Philemon braunching out in boughes and twigs before hir eyes.
And as the Bark did overgrow the heades of both, eche spake
To other whyle they myght.

— Arthur Golding, *Metamorphosis*

Euclid's Harmonics is the product of the sixth Café Writers Commission. The Commission is supported by Kate Birch and Dominic Christian and held in conjunction with poetry webzine *Ink Sweat & Tears* whose print section publishes the pamphlet. Each winner receives £2000 and 100 copies of their collection.

The judges of the 2014 Poetry Pamphlet Commission were Kate Birch, Chris Gribble (Chief Executive of Writers' Centre Norwich) and poet Helen Ivory. Chris recused himself from the final deliberations over Jonathan Morley's proposal because of their joint connection with the Centre.

Jonathan Morley's poetry won an Eric Gregory Award in 2006 and his work was included in *The Allotment* (Stride, 2006) and *Voice Recognition* (Bloodaxe, 2009). He has performed from his pamphlet *Backra Man (*Heaventree, 2008) and the accompanying jazz CD at festivals around the world. He contributed essays to *The Oxford Companion to Black British History* (2007) and has edited the work of numerous Caribbean writers, both historical figures and contemporaries, as well as programming and producing theatre shows, concerts and outdoor arts festivals for The Drum in Birmingham. He is currently the Programme Director at Writers' Centre Norwich.

And here the groaning shelves Philemon bends

— Alexander Pope

Local colour. Work in all you know.

— James Joyce

Contents

Preface: the Holland Apparatus

James Shapiro's recent book *1606* includes a chapter on the abortive uprising in Warwickshire that accompanied the Gunpowder Plot (Faber & Faber, 2015). It's exciting stuff: warhorses "thundering" across the county, bridges chained up and munitions procured for the defence of Stratford-upon-Avon. Shapiro outlines William Shakespeare's network of "intimate" relationships with a procession of local figures – John Grant, George Badger, Mrs Quiney, Alexander Aspinall, old Fulke Greville, Bartholomew Hales – who were caught up in the events, some as lawmakers and militiamen, and some who conspired to hoard the illicit "massing relics" of suppressed Catholicism. It's in keeping with his project of writing a Shakespeare biography that seeks to part company with the elusive Will of the dreaded secondbest bed, and instead contextualises the plays to make Shake-scene a sort of Aeolian Harp of his times. "Shylock chimes with the jewbaiting that followed the hanging and quartering of the queen's leech Lopez... Hamlet and Macbeth with the coming to the throne of a Scotch philosophaster with a turn for witchroasting... Warwickshire jesuits are tried and we have a porter's theory of equivocation", as Joyce has Stephen Dedalus summarise the method in *Ulysses*.

Events veer between Kenilworth and Warwick, the quiet country lanes and thatched villages, overlaid with motorways, where I used to ramble as a student, but it strikes me there's a Coventry-shaped hole in the narrative; it's mentioned once, as the young Princess Elizabeth is sent there for her safety from nearby Coombe Abbey, seat of the Haringtons, but there is no sense of a city, no sense of how the Stratfordians, or Shakebag himself, might have engaged with its merchants and scholars. Although fallen on hard times since the decline of the local wool trade, Coventry had once been great. Dr Philemon Holland, the "Translator Generall in his age", who had moved there after marrying in the 1580s, characterised it in his 1610 edition of William Camden's chorographical bestseller *Britannia* as "in the foregoing age, growing wealthy by clothing and making of Caps, it was the onely Mart and City of trade in all these parts, frequented also and peopled more than ordinarily a midland place". It would have teemed with working people, been rife with religious disagreement.

Holland (1552-1637) was, among other occupations, physician to the Harington family; as Charles Whibley imagines the scene, "Down the stately avenues, less stately then, but already avenues, went Philemon Holland to the unruined Kenilworth... to the enduring splendours of Warwick. Wherever he paid his visits he was welcome, for was he not the scholar of whom all the country was proud? Was he not the kindly physician, who healed not for money, but for healing's sake?" Born in Chelmsford, the son of a Marian exile, Holland had studied at Cambridge under John Whitgift (later Archbishop of Canterbury), going on to supplement his job of usher, or assistant teacher, at Coventry's Free School by translating over several decades a voluminous collection of

Ancient Greek and Roman texts: Livy's *Roman Historie* (1600), Pliny's *Naturall Historie* (1601), Plutarch's *Morals* (1603), Suetonius' *Twelve Caesars* (1606), Ammianus Marcellinus' *Roman Historie* (1609) and Xenophon's *Cyrupaedia* (1632) as well as producing one of the last hard-word dictionaries from Latin (1615) and the definitive English text of the aforementioned *Britannia*. John Taylor the infamous "Water-Poet" corroborates Holland's renown in his *Pennylesse Pilgrimage* of 1618:

Through plashes, puddles, thick, thin, wet and dry
I travell'd to the city Coventry
There Master Doctor Holland caus'd me to stay
The day of Saturn and the Sabbath-day

What must they have made of one another, the rambunctious pamphleteer and the tireless translator who (as his great grandson recalled to Anthony à Wood) "was always of a peacable and quiet Spirit, and hated Contention as a Serpent"?

Holland states his ambition as a translator in his Preface to Livy: "I frame my pen, not to any affected phrase, but to a meane and popular stile... if the sentence be not so concise, couched and knit togither as the originall, loth I was to be obscure and darke: have I not Englished everie word aptly?" I read "meane" in its sense of average, to refer to a broad-based appeal (as in *Antony and Cleopatra*, "they take the flow o' th' Nyle / By certaine scales i' th' Pyramid; they know / By th' height, the lownesse, or the meane, if dearth / Or Foizon follow...") but by Victorian times, the usual critical response was to denigrate either the meanness or the prolixity of Holland's prose. Even at the time of writing, it seems the very act of translating a classical author into a more vulgar tongue was disapproved of in some quarters, and in his Pliny, Holland returns to the fray: "It is a shame (quoth one) that *Livie* speaketh English as hee doth: Latinists onely are to bee acquainted with him: As who would say, the souldiour were to have recourse unto the universitie for militarie skill and knowledge; or the schollar to put on arms and pitch a campe. What, should *Plinie* (saith another) bee read in English, and the mysteries couched in his books divulged: as if the husbandman, the mason, carpenter, goldsmith, painter, lapidarie, and engraver, with other artificers, were bound to seeke unto great clearks or linguists for instructions in their severall arts." The "meane", as Sophie Chiari notes in a recent essay, is Protestant; it unshrouds the Latin mysteries preferred by Catholicism. But Thomas Fuller's appraisal of Holland, in *Worthies of England*, that "the Books alone of his Turning into English will make a Country Gentleman a competent library for Historians" seems something of a backhanded compliment, while Pope's *Dunciad* stacked the "solid Learning" of Holland's weighty folios into an altar of Dulness: "The Classicks of an Age that heard of none". The fascination of the eighteenth-century antiquaries with Holland's relics – "the one poore Pen, made of a grey Goose quill" with which he is said to have translated Plutarch, his signet ring and its anagram upon his name in Greek – speaks, I suspect, of the Restoration backlash against Puritanism: the counter-revolutionary harping upon an old Catholic theme.

Poor old Dr Holland seems to have been turned down promotion in much the same way as he was gradually rubbed out from literary history: offered the post of headmaster at the Free School in Coventry after twenty years' service, too old and frail to discharge his duties, he fell upon hard times in the 1630s, when the Master of Magdalen College awarded him charitable benevolence, noting that "He translated diverse books, and for 60 years kept good hospitality, *Sit tota Coventria testis*, and by age being disabled to travel abroad and practise, and confined to his chamber, he is impoverished, and indebted, having had a great charge of children." There are records to suggest he was evicted from city-centre properties in the final years of his life. His modest epitaph, "a se ipso confectum", made by himself, riffs punningly on *Ecclesiastes*' "All go unto one place; all are of the dust, and all turn to dust again." It's a Shakespearean turn. But we want our biographers, translators, critics in the limelight, we want our Elizabethans to be glamorous: explorers, courtiers, martyrs, spies. Not humble ushers.

Holland wrote that "it is neither my hap nor hope to attaine to such perfection as to bring foorth somewhat of mine owne which may quit the pains of a reader; and much lesse to performe any action that might minister matter to a writer", yet the sections in his translation of Pliny on animal husbandry, on the rearing and keeping of deer, pigs, doves, the techniques whereof he would have been familiar, are small masterpieces of English prose, and selections from the tightly-wrought essays in his Plutarch's *Moralia* withstand the test of time. Drayton's *Poly-Olbion* and Jonson's *Masque of Blackness* allude to Holland's *Britannia* (interesting that both writers have links to Warwickshire), while there is, it seems to me, a tantalising echo in Shakerags' Sonnet 55 of his phrase "a little whereof standeth *Stoneley*, destroyed when the flaming broiles of Danish warres under King Canutus caught hold of all England" (the translation was well underway by the summer of 1609, when a letter from Holland to Camden exists). Then there is Holland the architect of language, the eighth most-cited author in the *Oxford English Dictionary*; and the doctor of the 1649 edition of the *Regimen Sanitatis Salerni*, which he translated, and of *Gutta Podagrica*, his son's 1633 treatise on gout (unsensationally they intervene "rather by meats... than by medicines", recommend moderation over surfeit and propose a daily "Regimen of exercise"). Nowadays he is forgotten almost entirely; he seemed the fitting starting-point for a loose poetic meditation on work, on transience, on neglect; on what it felt like to try and start a career as a writer in the frowned-upon, rained-upon West Midlands – that

> lucklesse Cage
> Wherein you have bin cooped all your age
> And spent your golden yeares,

as another son, the poet Abraham Holland, lamented Coventry became to his father.

The Silver Age

His class released, he guided us with care
round the drab art room crammed with crooked screens
and littered tables, pointing here and there
where joy's surprise surmounted frugal means:

— John Hewitt

1.

Picture him in the late '60s, the dashing schoolmaster
on the bus to work, the demolition crews moving in,
the Indian kids in his art room at lunch
humming village songs of seed and harvest,
stopping at dusk to paint
half a building gone during the day, whalebones jutting
around the cold ribbon of a canal, a bomb-pit's moon.
Forty years later:
pony-traps whirling like leaves across the common
and happiness is the sheen on a chestnut flank.
A continuum exists from the highest maîtres
in their grand tombs of art
to the local, the decorative, he teaches. You can find it
in wrought-iron fossils and rainforest fronds
fastening a Hillfields works,
in angels with feathery trousers prancing on the Warwickshire rood,
in the Green Man's ivy tongues spoiling a grey façade
or mottled glass long held in the AXA sarcophagus.
Journeymen, the imperative to make.
He eats their stories, pays tribute
like an oven on a winter night.

---

kingfisher skims his
Quality Street wrappers—   quick
   into the river

13

2.

Poetry is endless revision: trudging
through slush to check the facts
on a smoky evening
a fresh sheaf of impressions dealt from his sketchbook.
Perched in a high window
he has fixed boys at a snowball fight,
their darting movements
pinioned in watercolours to his card

as the glimpsed flash before blinking
leaves a spoor hanging on the retina:
shadows braceleting a snowy amphitheatre of the green
made livid by streetlamps' fluorescence,
arms thrown like streamers:
constellated, still and in motion.

---

let him eat of birds
of such that live in the hills
as Feldefares Thrushes Blackbirds—

up in the yew's dusky vaults   scarlet flashes
blackbirds feast   toss back her globed flesh

3.

I am privy to a selection, his volume's a life:
The Airman Apprentice. Fitzrovia. Delia,
their love
his best painting. Summers
caravanning, passing for French. Annalist,
ox-roast, mummers, bloodthirsty football games
and Coventry: the sequinned dresses, like candle-flames fed with copper
of a mela, swift sketching sitar-players and dancers,
flirting with the jewellery-women in Punjabi
then, becaw he's sitting still, wheeling to draw the caricaturist
over a schoolgirl's shoulder: weaselly, alive
in the act of creation.

Philemon drank the last of his soup and sat back at his desk. He had spent the afternoon constructing letters to various writer friends and acquaintances, some of whom would recognise him and others, better known, he had met briefly at some literary soirée or shoot, who should not be interested in the slightest: following up on the inevitable fumble for a business card, an endorsement, the postal address that arrives when you've fooled them into thinking you know their work, enclosing a poem for one, a little joke for another, news of a forthcoming event to the third. All contained preview copies of his first collection of poems, published as an elegant chapbook by a Warwickshire press, yet the biggest was to come and Philemon was aware he had dithered the afternoon away. The names glared *tomorrow* from the postal pile. His tallow guttered and darkness swelled at the window. Writing to the old man was a significant moment in his career: and this chimerical entity could soar or be broken on the back of an ill-judged word.

4.

Stoke, high summer. Pretty china scenes on barges,
chateaux in pine forests, summoning
some old Bohemian clan bringing
Wedgwood and Doulton
down the Midlands canals.
He knows the story, has charcoaled them
a thousand times in the snug,
faces dark concentration
jerking bow or solemn around the whistle,
painted them in proud bright panes like Cézanne.
Work fleeing the person, to decay in a different time.
One jade afternoon
he's greeted by each repairer, engraver,
dance caller, Punch and Judy man
sapphire and tawny as Arcady I observe him
busy at a hot Molly troupe lumbering,
crossed swords or staves signifying
mow and thresh
their bearskin costumes.

divided into two parts, the *Feldon* and *Woodland*,
that is, into a plain Champian, and a woody Country:

which parts, the River *Avon* running crookedly
doth after a sort sever one from the other

the River rumbling here and there among the stones
carrying both colour and taste of milke

with his streame making a milde noise
and gentle whispering

Maiden in the Map

Here's the place. Stand still. She is not hard to find:
Speed has spread a lacework of lanes over
the Amazon curves of my lover, who turns on waking.
Her legs are crossed at White Fryers,
her hip rests on Grayfriars Gate
and the wall at Gosford Streete runs
a hand along her ass; she slackens
Fleete Streete's leather bond
strapping one breast to a necklace of rivers
saying St Michael's is her navel
but a School throngs at her heart—
and reclines below me on a throw of the Chilesmore meadows
where I am dizzy as the samphire gatherer hanging
with basket to a chalk cliff, the folio not yet printed.

Strongman Thrush, bandy-legged, you've
divined beetles among
the magnolia's broken alphabet:
death might have pecked
and listened and sprinted like this—

The orbit of Philemon's mind was disturbed. At one pole was encamped a sombre, willowy girl who inspired an irredeemable sadness in his heart; at the other bounced a bright street urchin, new into his life, who had appeared sitting in a dark corner at his launch, watching like a knife. One stirred his spirit like a toad is the slow heart in the winter pond – beautiful resting jewel – but the other made him feel alive again, a sexy little thing with grey eyes that slid over and over your oceanic skin, and they celebrated the solstice with splashing and gripping and grunting, raising his cock like a crowbar when he remembered it. Against overwhelming sadness Philemon weighed newness, motherhood, her sweet songbird voice. It was a relatively straightforward project: the seizure of documents from sixty years ago involved writing to one or two professionals in the academic network to ask for their help, an act of collation and repackaging, one hoped to the old man's benefit, then publication – but the fuck was famous. At their third and last meeting he had famously disavowed ownership of the book, with an impatient "come Sieglinde, let's go eat *chinoise*," to his wife, a tall, broad-shouldered Dane who did sterling duty as his bodyguard and literary agent.

17

Whittawer

for Tony Owen

Rogation-tide and you can choose
from a weighty Ariel in blue tattoos
an out-of-work Falstaff trading sweat for beer
or a lamppost *Juliet* SHANK *Romeo*.
Collapsed gravestones, moss obscuring their facts
an afternoon rubbed bright by the April wind.

Where tourists are corralled up Sheep Street to overpriced cafés
blossom stencilling speech bubbles overhead
we muscle like critical swans into the pale chapel
where once a whittawer paid his men two shillings,
ymages tumbling Escheresque above the nave
their scrubbing and *defasyng* unmarked still

Song 13 (Drayton Dub)

dowager Arden, elegant cheekbones
haughty in stature, her woodkerns flown

once stretched Trent to Severn
bronze torsos   gestating the seasons
tearing her emerald gown

THE BOAR HAS FLED, AND THE DUN COW
Greville hides in a village churchyard

Coventry forgets her Philêmon
not fit for humans now

your money is worthless
your bright maidens like corn to the scythe
laments old woman Arden

her hamadryads gone, gone
to the ships   to Guinea or Spain

Tymoteuš White Rat by yon canal
hoodie shadowing yr scowl
flat against concrete grey as bones
drizzle hissing in yr headphones

dubstep tumping in yr brain
where grey water skank w/ brummagem rain
bomber's moon like a basketball
yr tail uprooted copper cable

gunmetal-dark under railway bridge
Tymoteuš White Rat cool as a fridge
glimmering beneath an underpass
sandblast off nex time I pass

19

Usher

When wastefull warre shall Statues ouer-turne
And broiles roote out the worke of masonry

1.

Found you: "Jeffrey Woods Cross", now a scruffy roundabout
where African children go shiny in red uniforms
and HAZUKIAH is painted the traffic-light colours of Jah

then stepping out of the archives to trace your walk home
among the swineherds of Swan Lane
from the Old Free School by the LEARNING ZONE

four hundred years and a stone's throw from my house:
the squall's bite is in the grey air, light pools like yolk
at Cooke Streete Gate, squat as its olifaunt

Pomegranates and coriander on the wriggling street,
knots of Kurds, students garishly dressed. They do not see
half-wild pigs drinking at Swanswell Pool

in a painting by van de Poll
elixir veining throats and spines with gold.

2.

This city will ignore my book for you
as it ignored your books in turn,
your herbarium, the pasture, the sheltering elms and willows

the outlying schoolrooms pulled down
and a street named after Club Foot Hales
run over the meadow, over your house, in Victorian boomtime

the damp-spotted library used already for kindling:
a work on the Egyptian Hieroglyphics
a manuscript of Lydgate's Occleve's Poems, gilded and painted

the works of St. Ignatius, the works of St. Chrysostom
Livy's works, the works of Luther and Melanchthon
the works of King James, and Peter Charron on Wisdom

the Four Evangelists, in Saxon and English
the Treasures of the Latin Language
Ecclesiastical Music, written on parchment, around the time of Edward IV

a manuscript of Irish Poetry
Lambard's Perambulations in Kent
one hundred versions of the Lord's Prayer

a specimen of the same Prayer, in forty languages, with other books
in the Spanish, Italian, French, Russian, Belgic, Welsh and Irish languages
and two ancient wooden calendars

Plutarch's Lives (the Monk of Bury's translation)
Dante, with the Commentary of Sansobinus
the Holy Bible, in vellum, above five hundred years old:

the Renaissance flushed down the sewer.

3.

Waiting, waiting for the stony librarian and the elfin librarian to agree
on a policy for surrendering your early editions,
waiting for money for the train to London

for your dictionary of seven thousand Englished phrases,
waiting where the river hunts beneath the Burges
where the School's flank stretches boatlike above the RAMLA takeaway.

Down by the hand car wash, by the techno club
back of the MOTOR MUSUEM— high corrugated fence only
but green fists bubble around a hoarding— garden— yours?

I arks in the pub bordering on the yards (those Rood Lane tenements
you'll occupy with Magdelene Carpenter at the end)—
the entry is the neighbour's, ask next door—

waiting for Mr. Khan, corpulent and pinstriped—
the chipboard, the hatch, the padlocks
not his— and not the Council's. Christians,

they have their Cathedral, now they want
an overflow church. I need
to keep my premises clean, the meat halal.

We worship same god, but Muslims
prepare food differently, I can't cook next to a church,
I ask them, make it safe for two hundred Muslims,

I will turn it into a mosque, I send in volunteers,
clean out the pigeons and the mouse, they say
we'll meet three months after, Mr. Khan— nothing.

At street level the grilles are worn to lace,
a crack runs up the rib of the old chapel-heart
wide as my arm and as I lean to listen
sand crumbles like empires under my hand.

Biblio

upstairs your mingle mangle
leathery books
fingertip-soft pages
and your voice at last

they that thirle or boare throughs perles

in the vault
handwriting craves
to long swaying lines
on curling   yellow like bark the parchment shores

to eye a woman wiftly as having a wanton desire to her

stone heads   scratchd names
scripts neat
crabbed
broke

lurcher or devourer
the slit or clist in the neb of a penne

life preserved in a Lexicon
LATINO-ANGLICI PARALIPOMENA

hoarie full of grey haires
the pan seethes and wallops
God send you many scholars
to bubble or cast up bubbles   as urine in the urinall

mine

inward and hollow writhing   the hair crisped   curled   artificially
wax lither and hartlesse
a pedlar or one that hucketh
when in anger   teeth dash   gnash one   another

all my paines hath beene
to purge it from infinite absurdities
committed in precedent impressions

.

Witch-marks

So is it evident the Gout is a griefe

September, when sycamores wear red ruffs.
Tossed pennies in the road's black train.
Gout, you are the hunchbacked king, the gleam
of watching flint, the dark suit: speech.

GOUT: yam theevish serpenticall Owd Hob
glutting all ink from the woodcut
given much to scoffes and belly-cheere
capering on rachitic goaty legs:

as the ach in the fingers is called Chiragra
the ach in the knees is called Gonagra
the ach in the hips is called Sciatica
in the anckles (some terme) Talia Talaria—

Hob leaking humours, blood and spunk and piss
onto the faggots— remember well-wishers running in
with gunpowder in a bag, suicide belts.
Shug skinning his teeth near the old deer-gate.

Arre at the last Elizabethan, theefe-in-the-night:
it matters not which way the head lieth
so the heart be right— water eluding—
embroidered tent of ears and eyes—

   I is DesicCat man
    Dat is mah fuckries
    I cum fram King's Nahtan
   Dat is mah end—

You'll only leave a couple of orphans hanging:
Elizabeth, William, Compton, Abraham
are food now only for antiquaries.
The mason's chisel angles through marble

and Anne, Anne Bot, Staffordshire miss
lost like footprints in Danish snow
where Blackamores skidded and splashed quadrilles.
History is tangential, ephemeral, flesh.

the Moone is a planet Fœminine,
tender and nightly, dissolveth

the blood in men doth encrease
or diminish with her light

she putrifieth by her influence
pierceth and entreth effectually

she thaweth yce, and with moistening breath
enlargeth and openeth all things

out of Pontus the sea alwaies floweth
and never ebbeth againe

Epitaphium Doctoris Hollandi

Totus terra fui, terraque totus ero

February is a good month to warrant:
teeth of the wind in the leafless trees, in the eighty-fifth year of your age.
The grave you hack in supple fourteeners
a sombre and limewashed room,
realisation of all that is held at last
in the sepia boule of the skull.
Una fides votic haec est: without jazz,
bright glassware, sans epicure and feasting,
just eternal discoursing (newly robed).
Your sole companion in the senile years
a parchment-skinned Muse, faltering now—
she too shall be released and you
hold court together folded like hands
in all earth's closed book

26

Bottom's Dream

Turns them to shape, and gives to airy nothing
A local habitation and a name

So we play it like mas', Oberon as Cap'n
Jack Sparrow, Titania a dance-
hall fatty squeeze into leggings and bling;
we imp crew in ultraviolet warpaint
slinking around this box-bare studio.
De fole stan' empty in de drungèd fiel'
An craws are fatted wid de murrion flark!
outside dogs howling at gangsta-rap bass,
Lucky Strikes asterisking the sultry dusk.

I dream of your namesake, Begorrat's
Tisbe, poisoner (*Lord in this water*
wash all my sufferation away—)
questioned, hanged, decapitated, spiked,
her husband, earless Felix, forced to watch;
hard-handed men, now broken dauphins and kings
carried raving to fire-pit or scaffold.
Bouqui, Pierre François, Louis Quatorze,
Antoine, Manuel the Ibo, La Fortune,
Yala and Youba, Aubinot, Icare
who flew too close, the failed sorcerers.

---

when men also are sound asleepe
the dull nummednes thereby gathered

she casteth the old coat that cloggeth
become dim and dark, shee rubbeth

Fox laieth his eare close to the yce
guesseth thereby how thicke the water is frozen

out of Pontus the sea alwaies floweth
and never ebbeth againe

Drupe

for Gilad Atzmon

Once a year we go to the olive groves,
the paperwork laborious, the guards surly
and unkind, in spite of the mellow sky
to spread tarpaulins under the gnarly trees
and climb stepladders, to stroke and tap
the branches, so fruit rains to the cause
though the basalt press sleeps unanointed now
and chickens no longer roost in the crooks.
This year the old trees crouch in slow grief,
their branches torn and strewn around like limbs
and stapled to the trunks, a surah of Moses:
O my people, enter the holy land—
as in Arden, Rosalind's heart clenching
to a stone fist at the clumsy love poems.

In Gaza they're destroying tunnels, where
the Palestinians come and go in darkness
and smuggle things in too: it's a prison.
Samer dances for his children while bombs
crash two blocks away. Rafeef whispers fairytales:
sunlight jewelling in the apricot orchards
and ripening hate washed from children's eyes.

Here the wind will distract us again
from vigil, candles lit outside labyrinths,
an appeal for blankets at the Lebanese
or the cold drip of news. Banshee, grief-drenched
on my roof, pulling out oil-black fistfuls
of her hair. The streetlamps watching like gangsters.
"This is Paradise, my little prince—"

A Deaf Yout Inna Russells Bakery

Kid Rain reasoning with the Lozells Road, so the counter
unusually busy, even for lunchtimes, when you enter
gesticulating at the blackboards in old-skool semaphore,
all wrists and elbows, with a bedraggled white translator;
and when she has signed for you what coin is needed, you might choose
to investigate your snapper for bones in these steamed-up windows,
crumble a dumplin's doughy boulder to rockstones,
the gravy catch a fire inside you like sun is rising—
but you will never hear the cavernous boom of Rastaman demanding
his lunch, nor the subversive muttering
in the queue: *a mans be quicker— mi go get mi hair cut, ke ke ke—*
Where mi thigh an frie?— never go hear one of the ageing sisters swish back
the chain curtain, enumerate your order like a roll-call:
fish tea, stew chicken with food, sexy juice, festival—

angry man, take a NutriBullet to it,
whizz up Cucumbers, Gourds, Lettuce, Endive, suchlike
to cool the fountaine of heat, which is the heart:
for a boost, Violets, Tamarinds or Rose Oil
will balance your choler to the greenness of leek blades:
that mayor who slew an alderman whose greyhounds
attacked his spaniel, such a Coventry tale
may not have realised he was rusting inside
like a stalled factory, like a disused pit,
like a Socialist Party pamphleteer
amidst knock-down music pubs,
the Jailhouse, the Beer Engine, the Hope & Anchor
burning to fight—

Link

WHAT YA LOOKING AT
SHIT FACE

Sunday, a little girl in a white cotton dress,
her hair in braids, jumping on a low brick wall
top of Chain Walk, a prayer of chicken and thyme
near its conclusion and here against scaffolded shell,
the old Crocodile Works, glossy saints, ten feet high
JUSTICE and SOWETO mark the length of her journey:
back when the price of a Negro was one Birmingham gun
warehouses spring up by the canal the Council now pull down
then *Bremichem, full of Inhabitants, resounding*
with hammers and anvils, come larger and hungrier:
rum or coffee to fix you up, tobacco to cure the rheums
sugar to sweeten conversation in every front room
limes for scurvy sailor-boys, timber for faster ships
trinkets for the egungun, Newfoundland codfish
new markets for wool-cloth, the northern cities growing
daffodils nodding their heads
engineers with know-how to build railway bridges
landscape gardens for the rich in their fancy houses
all underwritten by credit from the Barclays and the Lloydses—
Rea, strait-jacketed in her brick coffin, forgets
everything and only names, River Street,
a boarded-up Floodgate Tavern in emerald script, recall:
long before the late-night blues, before Haile Selassie
before we bun a cally and prowl like dread lionesses
was nuttn ere but the field and the forge,
white folk eking out hard lives on the edge of Arden.
Let them not divide us with the gleam of gold and goods.
Shoulder to shoulder we stand, we are stronger together.

30

Rahtid!

Migrating here to work I'd assumed rahtid to mean a bad-word
like rass, raasclart, or maybe related
to the iyal raaa— really? right?
mi hear roar by a skettel on a bus one night
or else an address,
Ras, one of those lionlike Rastafar*I*an names
invoke in frustration— but Cassidy & Le Page
send I back to King James'
overwroughted, over-embellished, stressed
and this Jamaican editorial office
with its soon-come deadlines, its Augean mess of papers
momentarily recalls Jacobean scholars
wrangling, page after hard-wrought page
at Westminster and Oxford and Cambridge
so bibles could be ship in hundreds across the sea,
their words entrusted to new colonies
be stolen, worked hard, held through the amber centuries
before finding they route back: to Birmin'm, to we

Fam

Tenda Ladie   MadEm   Eu4ic   HYPZE

"He says he *loves* me! He says I'm his *babymother*—"
phoning from an icy bus shelter at nine o' clock one November night
her voice bursting with pride, this skinny teenager with a pram
at some battle won, paternity acknowledged,
the thin security of CSA payments and sporadic contributions
towards birthdays and classes and Christmas if a works go well;
maybe she will be driven once more in his bimmer
or at least win an occasional Saturday night's freedom to roll
those hips in a bashment, flaunt her chocolate thighs—
mi just hear the panic catch at her throat, see silver swelling
like Africa earrings in the ends of her eyes
when another unexpected doctor's bill comes due
when another trainers or school uniform is outgrown
or when the chile sixteen and gone missing one eveling, in these times
of turf and postcode of war over words, walls, tribes—

---

the Swan pressing Leda's face into black mud
firedrakes drinking at the pitch-lake in the sky

32

Precious

On Nigeria's fiftieth birthday you email me first
spelling out your delicious many-syllabled name,
transporting me back ten years to when online was new
and a hanged journalist's statement written in jail
fed flames of justice in the heart of a young student;
fifty years, to when that dead man's tribe of weavers, fishermen
who had not changed except time changed around them
were cast as extras in the national story, judged
on the length of a nose or the relative palette of skin;
four hundred years, huddled in the stinking holds
as our world ended in the mineral grasp of the sea,
shit, screaming, deaf gods, the courage it took to raise
warm hands to a face, trace an alphabet in another's scars—
the horror seems nothing when set against your story
of foster-parents, cracked skin, those torpid Oxfordshire villages
on this day of bright sunshine and trembling yellow leaves.
Precious, I cannot comprehend, can only imagine
shapes your eyes and smile might make, shining in darkness
like rhombi of moonlight playing on a river's night-skin
and watch you draw the breathless world into your dance.

Philémon, a comicall Poet who teaches them rhetoric and writes on Thursday and Saturday afternoons, distracted by their faint canticles drifting across the watermeadow. English polyphonic, not unpleasing. Chiasmus. From March to November he is up at five to stretch, plank, squat and gather the juiciest herbs. Hypozeugma, mesozeugma. Hops, fumitory, old must of sage or thyme and quick of mint. A chirping or creeking of grasshoppers. Auxesis, Latin amplificatio, that's his mode. Hendiadys, the trick of twins. Famous for his doggish and unsociable behaviour, Dugdale! He tests their enthusiasm for words, sometimes notes their slang; encourages them as glossarists. Tricolon. Better harmonise than tawse. Soon the raspberries will flower in a million splayed hands. And all those years of joyless Corporation stooges, of politricking churchmen and their bloody nostalgia. Moulton and Purefoy, the writs of entry for the Middle Wastes and Calves Close. Yet who'd have thought young Dugdale— energetic but directionless— would historicise the whole damn county, a little Camden in the making. They say when he was born a swarm of bees. Regular Mid-Land Souldier that one—

Coventry Boys

one pie-shaped boy
in sky-blue T
jumps from the car's
passenger door
to flob on buz
while his father's
hid by the buz
almost knocks me

three rat-face boys
playing cricket:
foot-length of dowel
fistful of gravel
end of the road

six little Sikhs
pelt like foals
uphill from Swanswell
their heads are boats
the sky scrap metal

name
Arthur Genders
Builders Merchants
off Clovelly Row
Kev's Chop Shop
Beautiful Cuticles
the Sky Bleu Batch Bar (the Kurdistan Hand Car Wash)
Moira's Wet Fish
the city names
the sanctuary
of those who turn the lathes
those that drive the buzzes
those who make fins
that spin the propellers
to fly the jet engines
rolling the king
back to his boys
those who make screws

of certain length
and are sold along
with their machine
those who mend
great leather belt
hundreds of yards
on the factory floor
to synchronise the men
the screeching and strafing of metal
thing strange in these days

I'll take you bab up the Ollybrush Balti
and I will buy you chicken jahlfrezi,
we'll listen to the radio all night long
its mingle of Bollywood and Quran
and I'll ignore the intercom's commands
for your eyelashes curl like their melodies:
the only way to travel, beetling down
the Hill, the drilling engine shouts to roar
then we're swooping like Whittle on the town
panels shaking, the tom-tom's crosshair
trained upon the point our chariot was born
precisely as German radio-beams
flickring along our moonlit rivers:
the Burges— the Birdcage— the Campbell— Club Release
and what of the abuse, the vomit-stained
seat, quick-legged lads in the entry, the
Poles encroaching on the licensed strip?
I carry a kirpan, and at my call
each sore-arsed cabbie in the Foleshill Road
shall be at my back, nimbler than the police
whose cast-off gadgets our quick sons can doctor!

NOTE. 'The Silver Age' was written for the eightieth birthday of the painter Colin Dick, a Royal Academician working in the regionalist-impressionist tradition who settled in Coventry, where he would find employment as a schoolteacher for many years, during that city's period of post-war reconstruction. John Hewitt's sonnet 'Art Room in a City School', dedicated to Dick, can be found in the Ulsterman's *Collected Poems*, edited by Frank Ormsby for Blackstaff Books, while the line "like an oven on a winter night" comes from a *kabta* or praise-poem written in Punjabi by Dick's "soul-friend" Channon Singh Chandhu (the notorious "Dr. Chan"), and translated by the present author with S. K. Dhaliwal:

ਤੇ/ਨ੍ਹ /ਤੇ

Renowned in his lifetime, Colin Dick
ticking like a clock, that's Colin Dick
who made five paintings of Chan,
his very best friend: Colin Dick.

When the Punjab tears itself apart
the greatest grief is Colin Dick's—
yes, he will be at the front
holding truth's flag high: Colin Dick.

Deeper than the sky
the soul of Colin Dick;
lighting the darkness with his presence,
sending it far away: Colin Dick.

Bring a million starving Ethiopians,
he will help them all: Colin Dick,
his gift as a maker
surpasses all artistry: Colin Dick.

He chomps hot coals
like an oven on a winter night: Colin Dick,
always first in line
to make life good: Colin Dick.

Write, Pen, and praise him,
the unique Colin Dick!

During the heyday of The Heaventree Press in the late twenty-noughties praise-poems for "Mr. Dick" enjoyed something of a vogue in Coventry, with former pupils now grown middle-aged and new poets, inspired by his attendance at their events and warmed by his generosity of sketchbooks and memories, vying to pay tribute to this waterfall-bearded, tweed-jacketed lecturer manqué who would hurtle his wheelchair across the most alarming terrain in search of literary quarry as if still hurrahing upon the wild stallions and motor-cars of his youth.

But *we* see them all, the lines of force that hold the whole show
& they who know their secret, they are free— come & go
As you please, Sirmadamson, citizen of city-air, knower known.

One such we spied today, a lone wizard, roving eye, sat on a stool;
He chose his own lines, inhabitant of the boundary zone,
Catching the story-spirit in his talisman to make it dance!

— Barry Patterson

Your pages collect the minutiae of moments,
the country people of the central shires,
the mummers' plays and circus big top tents,
grey horses next to cracking gypsy fires.

— Michael McKimm

And pictures in the Herbert?
For a schoolboy, it was cool:
A real, proper artist—
Teaching at our school!

— Martin Brown

The "Tyger, with more than Blake-like glare" in Hewitt's poem testifies to the respect and affection in which Dick was held by Sikhs, while his "batik-rainbow wrought with candle grease; / the roughly scissored textures which contrive, / from hoarded scraps of fabric, to compose / an underwater world which seems alive / with hovering monsters" speak of the redemptive power of the imagination under adverse circumstances (a bombed-out city, the decline of British car manufacturing, the economics of austerity). It is hoped that the rhythms and imagery of 'The Silver Age' will similarly convey something of the man's energy to the reader, as witnessed by a friend of his twilight years:

Old painter, teacher, Punglish-speaker, beard
nest to escaped songbirds from Stow Fair— go!
wassail your cider-trees; make our sap burn.

For more information on Dick's life and work, see the biographical essay by Richard Yeomans, *Colin Dick: Seeing Life* (HobbsMclaughlin, 2011).

Acknowledgements

Thanks to James Byrne, editor of *The Wolf*, who first published several of these poems. Others appeared in *Dove Release*, David Morley's anthology celebrating ten years of the Warwick Writing Programme (Worple, 2011). Thanks to Helen Ivory and Martin Figura and their workshop group (Tiffany Atkinson, Joanna Guthrie, Andrea Holland, Matthew Howard, Andy McDonnell, Esther Morgan and Tom Warner) who, more recently, have commented usefully on drafts; also to Kris Connolly, David Dabydeen, Mukhtar Dar, Michael McKimm, Tony Owen, Sic'Nis, Chris Gribble and Sophie Scott-Brown; to my translators Cristina Babino (Italian) and Dirceu Villa (Brazilian Portuguese); and to Si Hayden for setting these poems to music. 'Song 13 (Drayton Dub)' won a place on the Polesworth Poets Trail in 2009 and is etched on a sculpture outside Polesworth Library in Warwickshire as a result; thanks to organiser Malcolm Dewhirst and judge Jane Holland. Several poems towards the end of the sequence were written at the invitation of Ronké Fadare to contribute to the libretto for her streetdance theatre performance *Chalk Circle*, which premiered at The Drum Arts Centre, Birmingham in 2011. Visiting Port-of-Spain, where I saw the Trinidad Theatre Workshop perform *A Midsummer Night's Dream*, was made possible through an Artists International Development Fund grant from Arts Council England in 2013. Thanks finally to Kate Birch and Dominic Christian for their generous sponsorship of the Café Writers Commission.

The idea to write about Philemon Holland took root at the University of Warwick when I stumbled across F. O. Matthiessen's essay in *Translation: An Elizabethan Art* (University of Harvard, 1931)— still the most detailed and sympathetic analysis of Holland's prose technique. It seemed extraordinary that this now all-but-forgotten "Translator Generall in his age" (the phrase is from Fuller's *Worthies*) had lived on my doorstep. Other sources of information I've consulted since have included Charles Whibley's introduction to Suetonius' *History of Twelve Caesars* (David Nutt, 1899) and E. H. Blakeney's 1911 introduction to the J. M. Dent selection from Plutarch's '*Moralia*', while the biographical picture is fleshed out by David Considine's 2004 entry on Holland in the *ODNB* (8095 coinages in the *OED*!) and supplemented by Thomas Sharp's *Illustrative Papers on the History and Antiquities of the City of Coventry* (compiled circa 1816, edited and printed in Birmingham by W. G. Fretton in 1871). Andrew Mealey at the Coventry History Centre and Coventry historian David McGrory each pointed me in the direction of interesting ephemera; it is to Coventry, and to Dr Holland's original texts (particularly his Pliny, Plutarch, Suetonius and Camden, and his Latin Dictionary) that I would signpost the reader whose curiosity is piqued by these brief decompositions.